WILD
BEARS

D0702324

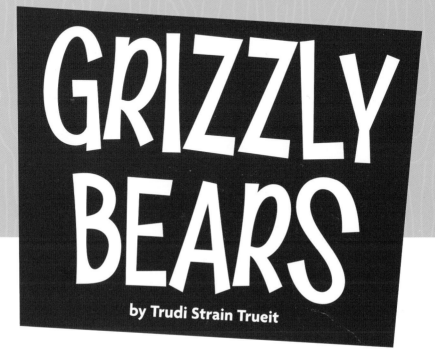

GRIZZLY BEARS

by Trudi Strain Trueit

WITHDRAWN

AMICUS HIGH INTEREST 🦴 AMICUS INK

Amicus High Interest and Amicus Ink
are imprints of Amicus
P.O. Box 1329, Mankato, MN 56002
www.amicuspublishing.us

Copyright © 2016. International copyright reserved
in all countries. No part of this book may be reproduced in any form
without written permission from the publisher.

Library of Congress Cataloging-in-Publication Data

Trueit, Trudi Strain, author.
  Grizzly bears / Trudi Strain Trueit.
      pages cm. -- (Wild bears)
  "Amicus High Interest is published by Amicus."
  Summary: "Presents information about the grizzly bears of North
America, their habitats, and their amazing size and strength."-- Provided
by publisher.
  Audience: K to grade 3.
  Includes bibliographic references and index.
  ISBN 978-1-60753-775-5 (library binding)
  ISBN 978-1-60753-874-5 (ebook)
  ISBN 978-1-68152-026-1 (paperback)
  1. Grizzly bear--Juvenile literature. [1. Bears.] I. Title.
  QL737.C27T775 2015
  599.784--dc23
                            2014043615

Photo Credits: Randy Wells/Corbis, cover; davidrasmus/iStockphoto, 2,
20–21; seread/iStockphoto, 4; RONSAN4D/iStockphoto, 6–7, 22; Galyna
Andrushko/Shutterstock Images, 8–9, 23; John E Marriott/All Canada
Photos/Glow Images, 11; Antoni Murcia/Shutterstock Images, 12–13;
Stephen J. Krasemann/All Canada Photos/Corbis, 14–15; Roy Toft/National
Geographic Creative, 16; Kandfoto/iStockphoto, 19

Produced for Amicus by The Peterson Publishing Company
and Red Line Editorial.

Designer Becky Daum
Printed in Malaysia

HC 10 9 8 7 6 5 4 3 2 1
PB 10 9 8 7 6 5 4 3 2 1

TABLE OF CONTENTS

BIG BEARS

Grizzly bears are big. They stand eight feet (2.4 m) tall on their back legs. They can weigh more than 1,300 pounds (590 kg).

GRIZZLY FUR

Most grizzlies are brown. Some are dark brown. Others are a lighter tan color. Their fur has white tips. This can sometimes make the fur look gray.

Fun Fact
The word grizzly means "having gray hair."

MANY HABITATS

Grizzly bears live in North America. They have many **habitats**. Some live in forests. Others roam in **meadows**. They also live on mountains.

FOOD IN THE FOREST

Grizzly bears eat berries and plants. They dig for insects and roots. Strong muscles help them dig. Long claws help too.

Fun Fact
Grizzly bear claws are up to four inches (10 cm) long!

HUNTING AND FISHING

Grizzly bears also eat deer. They chase their **prey**. The bears eat fish too. They catch salmon in their jaws.

Fun Fact

Grizzlies are fast. They can run 35 miles per hour (56 km/h)!

A WINTER NAP

Grizzly bears eat lots of food.

They get ready to **hibernate**.

Grizzlies find a **den**. They rest all

winter. They don't eat or drink.

Fun Fact
A grizzly can lose 200 pounds (91 kg)
while it hibernates!

BEAR CUBS

Grizzly cubs are born during winter. The mother may not even wake up. She usually has two cubs. The babies sleep and grow in the den.

Fun Fact
Newborn grizzly cubs weigh less than a can of soda!

WAKE UP!

Grizzly bears wake in the spring. They leave their dens. The young cubs now weigh 20 pounds (9 kg). The mother teaches them to hunt and fish.

GUARDING GRIZZLIES

Grizzly bear habitats are in danger. Fewer grizzlies live in the lower United States today. Most live in Canada and Alaska. People are now working to protect grizzlies.

GRIZZLY BEAR FACTS

Size: 176–1,321 pounds (80–600 kg),
39–110 inches (100–280 cm)

Range: North America

Habitat: forests, meadows, mountains

Number of babies: 2

Food: fish, berries, deer

WORDS TO KNOW

den – a hole or cave where an animal lives

habitats – places where plants or animals naturally live

hibernate – to pass the winter in a resting state

meadows – grassy areas often near rivers

prey – animals hunted for food

LEARN MORE

Books

Brett, Jeannie. *Wild about Bears*. Watertown, Mass.: Charlesbridge, 2014.

Kolpin, Molly. *Grizzly Bears*. Mankato, Minn.: Capstone, 2012.

Miller, Debbie S. *Grizzly Bears of Alaska*. Seattle, Wash.: Sasquatch Books, 2014.

Websites

Katmai National Park & Preserve, Alaska—Bear Cam
http://www.nps.gov/katm/photosmultimedia/brown-bear-salmon-cam-brooks-falls.htm
Watch bears catch fish!

National Geographic—Grizzly Bears
http://animals.nationalgeographic.com/animals/mammals/grizzly-bear
Learn about grizzly bears and watch bear videos.

INDEX

31901056960240